FEB 1 4 2011

Fun Adventure Crafts

Haunted House

Adventure

Crafts

Anna Llimós

Enslow Elementary
an imprint of
Enslow Publishers, Inc.
40 Industrial Road
Box 398
Berkeley Heights, NJ 07922
USA

http://www.enslow.com

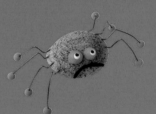

tents

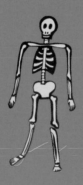

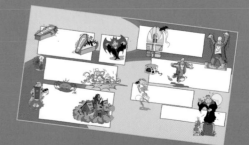

Coffin

Materials

* clay
* plastic spoon
* poster paint
* paintbrush
* rolling pin (Ask permission first!)
* plastic knife

3. For the lid, flatten out a piece of clay with the rolling pin. Place the lid on top of the coffin as a guide. With the plastic knife, cut the sides of the lid to fit the coffin.

1. Mold the clay into a rectangle. Use a plastic knife to cut it into the shape of a coffin.

2. Use a plastic spoon to hollow out the inside of the coffin.

4. Decorate the lid any way you wish, using clay or paint. Let it dry.

5. Decorate the coffin any way you wish, using clay or paint. Let dry.

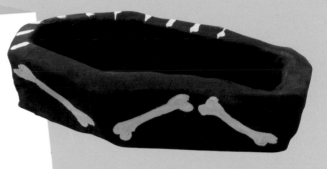

Is anyone in there?

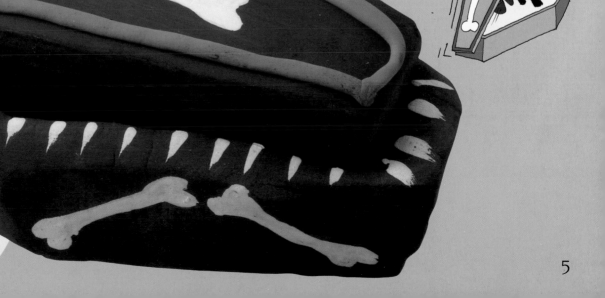

1. Roll out a long, thick piece of clay to make the vampire's body. Use a ball of clay for the head. Attach the head to the body with a toothpick.

Materials

* clay
* rolling pin (Ask permission first!)
* plastic knife
* toothpick

2. Use a plastic knife to make the mouth. Make eyes, a nose, ears, eyebrows, and fangs with clay. Attach the eyes, nose, ears, eyebrows, and fangs to the head.

Welcome!

3. Roll out a small piece of clay and flatten it. Wrap it around the neck to make a shirt collar.

4. For the hair, cut small pieces of clay and stick it on the head.

Vampire

I sleep in the coffin!

5. Choose two pieces of clay, each one a different color. Flatten the pieces with the rolling pin. Place one on top of the other. Roll the pin over the two pieces to join them together.

6. With the plastic knife, cut the flattened clay into the shape of a cape. Wrap the cape around the vampire.

Candles

Materials

* paper towel tubes
* toilet tissue tubes
* poster paint
* clay
* toothpicks
* paintbrush

1. Paint the paper towel and toilet tissue tubes any color you wish. Let dry.

2. Roll out some long, thin pieces of clay. Place them on one end of each tube so that they cover the hole and hang down the sides.

3. Press the clay down onto the sides of the tubes to make it look like melting wax.

4. Make the flames by molding clay into raindrop shapes.

What a light!

5. Stick a toothpick into each flame and attach one to each candle.

9

Materials

- a cardboard grocery store fruit container, or paper bowl
- clay
- old toothbrush (Ask permission first!)
- masking tape
- craft wire
- poster paint
- white glue
- toothpick
- scissors

1. Use a paper bowl or cut out a bowl from a grocery store fruit container.

Scary Spider

The spider spins spooky webs!

2. With an old toothbrush, flick different colors of paint onto the bowl. Let dry. Use a toothpick to poke four holes into two sides of the bowl.

3. Cut four pieces of craft wire and pass one piece through a hole on each side of the bowl. Tape the four wires to the inside of the bowl.

4. Bend the wires to form creepy, crawly legs. Stick a small ball of clay onto the end of each leg.

5. Make eyes and a mouth out of clay.

I am the scariest spider!

6. Glue the eyes and the mouth to the spider. Let dry.

Mummy

Materials

* clay
* gauze
* toothpicks
* scissors

1. Model the body and the head of the mummy out of clay. Attach the head to the body with a toothpick.

2. Make the legs out of clay. Attach the legs to the body with toothpicks.

3. Make the arms out of two long, thin pieces of clay. Attach the arms to the front of the body with toothpicks.

I always trip on my bandages!

The clumsy mummy

5. Wrap the entire body in gauze. Tie knots to keep the gauze in place. Make sure to leave the eyes and the nose uncovered.

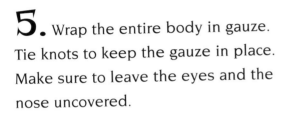

4. Mold the eyes and a nose out of clay. Attach the eyes and nose to the head.

Haunted House

Materials

- large tissue box
- poster paint
- scissors
- white glue
- markers
- paintbrush
- old toothbrush (Ask permission first!)
- string
- clear tape

1. Cut a large tissue box into three pieces, as shown in the photo.

2. Cut roofs from the flaps. If your box does not have enough flaps, draw the roofs as you wish and cut them.

3. Paint the walls of the house as you wish. Let dry.

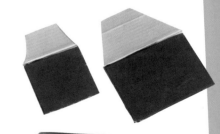

14

4. Paint the roofs. Let dry.

5. With an old toothbrush, flick paint onto the walls. Let dry.

6. Draw the roof tiles with a marker.

7. Glue the roofs and the walls together with some pieces sticking out from behind the others. Let dry.

The gloomy house

8. Draw and paint windows, doors, some grass, and a skull. Let dry.

9. On an extra piece of cardboard, draw and paint a lantern. Let dry. Cut it out.

10. Tape a piece of string behind the lantern and tape the other end to the house.

11. Finish decorating the house as you wish. Fold it at the seams so that it stands on its own.

Ghost

Materials

- clay
- tissue paper
- paper clips
- glue wash (1/2 white glue, 1/2 water)
- paintbrush
- white glue
- plastic wrap

4. Use clay to make the eyes and eyebrows. Glue them to the head. Let dry.

1. Make the ghost out of clay. This will be the mold.

3. Carefully separate the clay mold from the hardened tissue paper.

2. Wrap the clay mold in plastic wrap. Cover the plastic-wrapped clay mold with tissue paper. Brush over it with glue wash. The plastic wrap keeps the tissue paper from sticking to the clay. Do four or five layers of tissue paper and glue wash. Let dry overnight.

5. For the mouth, roll six small, long, and thin pieces of clay. Place them so two are horizontal and four are vertical. Glue it to the head. Let dry.

6. Make a ball out of black clay. Make a chain out of paper clips and attach it to the ball. Attach the chain to the bottom of the ghost through a tiny hole made by the same paper clip.

This ghost floats through walls!

Frankenstein

Materials

- clay
- two dowels
- two small screws
  (Ask permission first!)
- felt
- white glue
- scissors
- toothpick

6. Cut two equal pieces of felt for the shirt. Glue felt buttons onto one of the pieces. Let dry. Glue the two pieces of felt to Frankenstein's neck, one in front and one behind. Let dry.

20

1. Model Frankenstein's head and nose out of clay. Attach the nose to the head.

2. Use clay to make his hair, eyebrows, eyes, mouth, and ears. Attach the hair, eyebrows, eyes, mouth, and ears to the head. Use a toothpick to make creases in his forehead.

Everyone gets scared when I walk like this!

3. Make feet out of clay. Stick a dowel into each foot.

4. Cut two rectangles out of felt and wrap one around each dowel to make pants. Glue the pieces of felt closed. Let dry.

5. Attach the head to the dowels. Insert a screw into each side of the neck.

Materials

* small pear-shaped dried gourd
* clay
* toothpicks
* craft wire
* clear tape

1. Mix different colors of clay. Cover the dried gourd with clay, keeping the original shape but slightly stretching out the nose.

2. Mold four legs out of clay and attach them to the body.

3. Roll out a long, thin piece of clay for the tail. Attach it to the body.

4. Use a toothpick to make hair all over the body and to make the toes.

22

Scary Rat

Giant rats!

5. Make the ears and a nose out of clay. Attach them to the body.

6. Use clay for the eyes. Attach the eyes to the head. Cut the ends of some toothpicks and stick them into the mouth for the teeth. To make whiskers, tape some pieces of craft wire together at one end. Make a second bundle of craft wire. Stick one bundle into each side of the snout.

Skeleton

Materials

- card stock
- markers
- craft wire
- scissors
- clear tape
- white glue

What weak bones!

Again, I fall to pieces!

6. Tape the backs of all the different skeleton parts to the wire.

24

1. Shape the craft wire to make a head, body, legs, and feet. Leave a long piece of wire sticking out behind each foot. These will keep the skeleton standing on its feet.

2. Draw the bones. Draw the backbone on a different part of the card stock.

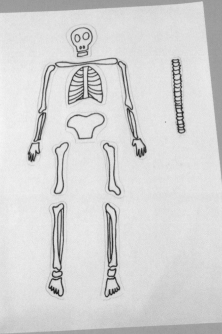

3. Color the inside of the bones with markers. Outline the bones in another color.

4. Cut the pieces out, leaving a border all around. Make sure the arms stay attached to the collarbone and to the rib cage.

5. Glue the skull to the top of the backbone. Glue the rib cage to the middle of the backbone, below the skull. Let dry.

Bat and Tombstone

Materials

+ corrugated paper
+ clay
+ craft wire
+ scissors
+ white glue
+ toothpick

1. Draw the body and the wings of the bat on corrugated paper. Cut them out.

2. Pass a piece of wire through the middle of the body, making a small hole. Bend the end of the wire a little to hold it in place.

3. Glue the wings to the body. Let dry. Make eyes with clay. Glue the eyes to the body. Let dry.

4. Form a tombstone out of clay.

26

It is the vampire in disguise!

I like to turn into a bat so I can fly.

5. For the grass and dirt, roll out a long thin piece of clay and wrap it around the bottom of the tombstone. Use a toothpick to make the blades of grass.

6. Decorate the tombstone any way you wish with clay. Stick the wire with the bat into the top of the tombstone.

Create your own story with all
the crafts in this book!

One night in Transylvania . . .

In the coffin lies a mysterious figure: the vampire, polite and well-dressed, but bloodthirsty.

A scary spider is almost crushed by a thousand-year-old creature—the mummy—who is always tripping on his bandages.

All these monsters wander through the dark night. They meet at the haunted house that is hidden by a spooky fog.

The vampire flies by the window, while the wandering ghost looks out the window.

The cowardly Frankenstein runs away from the scary rats that crawl at his feet. The rats have beady eyes and sharp fangs.

The skeleton always falls apart when he plays with his friend, the vampire.

We want to leave, but the vampire blocks our way out!

Who else dares to enter the haunted house?

Enslow Elementary, an imprint of Enslow Publishers, Inc.
Enslow Elementary® is a registered trademark of Enslow Publishers, Inc.

English edition copyright © 2011 by Enslow Publishers, Inc.

All rights reserved.

No part of this book may be reproduced by any means
without the written permission of the publisher.

Translated from the Spanish edition by Stacey Juana Pontoriero.
Edited and produced by Enslow Publishers, Inc.

Library-in-Cataloging Publication Data

Llimós Plomer, Anna.
[Crea tu. Casa del terror. English]
Haunted house adventure crafts / Anna Llimós.
p. cm. — (Fun adventure crafts)
Includes bibliographical references and index.
Summary: "Provides step-by-step instructions on how to make eleven
simple spooky crafts, such as a vampire, haunted house, mummy,
and more, and it includes a story for kids to tell with their crafts"—
Provided by publisher.
ISBN 978-0-7660-3730-4
1. Halloween decorations—Juvenile literature. 2. Handicraft—Juvenile
literature. I. Title. II. Title: Casa del terror.
TT900.H32L5413 2010
745.594'1—dc22
                              2009041462
ISBN-13: 978-0-7660-3731-1 (paperback ed.)

Originally published in Spanish under the title *Crea tu . . . Casa del terror*.
Copyright © 2008 PARRAMÓN EDICIONES, S.A., - World Rights.
Published by Parramón Ediciones, S.A., Barcelona, Spain.

Text and exercises: Anna Llimós
Illustrator: Àlex Sagarra
Photographs: Nos & Soto

Printed in Spain

122009 Gráficas 94 S.L., Barcelona, Spain

10 9 8 7 6 5 4 3 2 1

To Our Readers: We have done our best to make sure all Internet Addresses in this book were active and appropriate when we went to press. However, the author and the publishers have no control over and assume no liability for the material available on those Internet sites or on other Web sites they may link to. Any comments or suggestions can be sent by e-mail to comments@enslow.com or to the address on the back cover.

Read About

Books

Ritchey, Kate. *Creepy Crafts for Boys and Ghouls.* New York: Price Stern Sloan, 2006.

Sadler, Judy Ann. *The New Jumbo Book of Easy Crafts.* Toronto: Kids Can Press, 2009.

Internet Addresses

Halloween Crafts and Activities, Enchanted Learning
<http://www.enchantedlearning.com/crafts/halloween/>

Halloween Crafts, Kaboose.com
<http://crafts.kaboose.com/holidays/halloween/>

Index